What the Neighbors Know

Melanie McCabe

FUTURECYCLE PRESS
www.futurecycle.org

Copyright © 2014 Melanie McCabe
All Rights Reserved

Published by FutureCycle Press
Hayesville, North Carolina, USA

ISBN 978-1-938853-46-3

For my daughters, Shannon and Taryn

With gratitude to the Virginia Center for the Creative Arts and
George Mason University's Heritage Workshop

Contents

I.

Opened Houses... 9
This House.. 10
The Visitors.. 12
What the Neighbors Know... 13
In a Handbasket.. 14
Foresight... 16
Ballroom, Lee Plaza Hotel... 17
In Tongues.. 18
Imperatives.. 19
Without Snow... 20
Ghost Trees.. 21
But wait—.. 22

II.

Going Home.. 25
The Woman in the Window of My Old House................ 26
The Air Then.. 27
How It Began.. 28
She Fled.. 30
That Sanderson Show... 32
Missing the Train.. 34
Basement.. 36
The Boys of Woodlawn Park.. 37
Wednesday, Mt. Olivet... 38
Writing Memoir.. 39
Heirloom.. 40

III.

Goings and Stayings... 43
Ghosts... 44
The California Years... 45
Dreaming Alabama... 46
The Naked Days.. 47
Mercies... 48
Those Mothers.. 49
In These Woods... 50

Bound...51
Advice to a Mother..52
Your Oak..53
The Tree Leans In..54

IV.
With a Twang—Not a Whimper...57
What's Waiting..58
A Day in August...59
Checking the Weather in Barrow, Alaska..................................60
Settlement..61
Valediction...62
The Mail...63
In Boxes..64
These Walls..65
Synchronous..66
Creed...67
When You Come Home Now, You Will Need Directions......68

Acknowledgments...69

I.

Opened Houses

Anything is possible in an opened house.

There are walls, but not the walls you are used to.

Begin in a kitchen, humid with cinnamon
and late sun. Near a raised window
a chair is turned where someone lingered
to breathe in the forgiveness of boxwoods,
the orderly air. If you sit down here, you will
no longer be afraid of anything. This angle
of light will hold you inside it. Wait
and someone will walk through the door
who wants nothing you cannot give.

Among the bedrooms at the top of the stairs,
you will find one that belongs to you.
No curtain or carpet in it will remind you
of any room you have ever called your own.
That is how you will know it. No clocks
or knickknacks will clutter surfaces or break
the wood's long and lemon gleam. When you
peer into the mirror above the bureau, the face
that looks back at you will take your name.

Walk out at night when the swift black
erases you, when each yellow square fills
with what you are not. Then, if you can become
anything at all, it will be no more than the scent
of pendulous lilacs too heavy to rise above
a wet earth. There is mercy here; there is
no moon. Streetlamps are swallowed by
hollies and oaks. Every road you turn down
will glow with houses. Each glass passed

will give up its pantomime of lives.

Maybe one of them could be yours.

This House

The dirt alone is worth a half a million. Assessors say
land and building together would go for half again as much,

though the agent who sends calendars each Christmas spurns
cautious calculations. More, she says. Much more. She hasn't

seen the heave and buckle of the backyard walkway, the riddled
stairwell that spurts rain, the basement floor with its veneer

of mud. Nor has she tried to unlatch the cheap casement windows
that pop their catches and seals, then never after fully close,

or waited every spring for the resurrection of ants from
hidden colonies inside the walls. Still, this house is all

I have, so there is comfort in clinging to untapped wealth.
Sometimes I open doors to all the empty rooms to see if

they still exist, to watch dust motes swirl in the unexpected
air. There is space here now to house two lives

with space in between. There are unspoken territories.
There is a seam that runs between the original house

and its renovation. Unseen, but no less real for that.
Of all the dreams scrawled across any given night, among

the most common is said to be the dream of a house.
To imagine a house, Freud said, is to conjure one's body,

one's self, every room a metaphor. In my old dream, I
would remember a room I had forgotten existed, one

I could no longer ignore, either down a long hallway or
up a narrow stair. Though sometimes I would enter,

pleased to find this unused space I could claim as mine,
more often I was pulled to it by dread, a certainty

that what waited there was so harrowing, I must wake
to save myself. I have learned to live in this house with you,

both of us taking up only a part of it. Everyone knows that
a door is a symbol. But not every symbol needs to be opened.

The Visitors

Two mourning doves landed in tandem on the sill and stared
in at me. Just in case I didn't know my birds, one of them
opened its throat to offer that unmistakable grief, a kind

of calling card. They watched for a long time, black beads
unblinking, not even fluttering when I rose and moved closer.
This fearlessness was how I knew they had come as an omen.

I am not accustomed to the visitations of birds. I live life
indoors now, cumulus and light translated by panes. What wings
I see are only dark lines, moving over a blue I trust as sky.

I sensed their name was not an auspicious sign, though as a child
I thought it meant the time of day the doves preferred. And, indeed,
they came to me well before noon, before I had spoken a word,

spending, as I do, most of my hours alone. You were not there
to point them out to, to dismiss them as birds and nothing more.
They came and stayed an uncanny while, soft bodies shifting

side to side as they craned to see beyond the glass, to bring
their world into my closed one. I wanted them to mean something,
and they obliged. And, of course, there were two of them.

What the Neighbors Know

What the neighbors know is so small it might fit in my mailbox.
I wish they would put it there, unfolded, explicit, so I could be
certain of what they think they saw, the shaky black-and-white
reel they have colorized, the beginnings and middles cobbled
to find their way to the end.

No one will sign his name. Each separate letter will be cut
from newspapers, magazines, to keep the scales of knowing
unbalanced: *We have a piece of your life that we plan to torture
into something we recognize. We want more pieces. But
even then, we won't give you this one back.*

I once had all of their names but didn't keep them. Did they
keep mine? If we passed each other in some far-off town,
I wouldn't know them, though I have lived beside them
for nearly thirty years. Anonymity is a chosen loneliness,
but a secret in a cul-de-sac has a fleeting life.

Their eyes on my comings and goings, my middling tragedy,
are a kind of extortion, even if they never open their mouths.
If I do not give them reasons, they will think I had none.
If enough people paint me a heart of pitch, a rudderless
integrity, how could all of them be wrong?

Whatever the neighbors know, it is not enough, but the rest
of the story is not mine to tell. See me, then, half in shadow. Or
turn me, if you must, toward your lurid light. I will grow older,
quieter, until no one believes the tale you pin on me. I will wear
sensible shoes. I will outfox you by being too dull to be bad.

In a Handbasket

River cane would make a snug ride, or maybe
the black rushes of a Gullah sweetgrass,
but if I am going (and it seems as though

I might), I'd like to choose my own conveyance.
Pine needle or willow, cattail or bamboo—
if I went in a basket of bamboo, I could soothe

myself by chanting, softly, *Bamboo, bamboo,
bamboo,* for surely hell would seem
less sinister with that charm of b's on

my tongue. I thought at first, no matter
the method—whether coiled or twined, woven
or plaited—but it seems now that coils

would be a coward's way. Too easy
to burrow down and not look out on mayhem.
Better the burden of a weave with holes

for peering through—a wicker transport.
Certainly not the blindfold offered by those
Nantucket baskets with their scrimshawed lids;

I won't go quaking in shadow beneath a pretty
cover of etched ivory or bone. I should know
where I am going. Color is incidental. No need

for the stark white and black the Hopis wove
from sun-bleached yucca, the dark seed pods
of Devil's Claw. No pigments, dyes or paints,

for I prefer the earth tones of Indonesian vines,
or the bulrush grasses of the low country.
If I need a comfort on my way, give me

that scent of rattan that wafts from every
emporium of the Far East, or the clean balm
that lingers where dunes bar the sea.

Let this final going be the one act in my life
to which I give ample and deliberate thought.
Let me dally a long time, choosing.

Foresight

I know precisely what to do to avert disaster
and do not do it. My friends are wary,

prudent; I can read their minds.
Their blink of alarm, the way they bite

their lips, gaze down into the setting
moons of their fingernails, are signs

they do not intend to give, and yet
I see everything. It saddens me

to peer into the shadows of the wrong
road, and to take it anyway. On the insides

of my eyelids, I write screenplays to scare
myself, and come to no good in all of them.

I err on tip toe. I file extensions. No one
finds me because I hide behind my own door;

I finger the numbers of my cell phone,
but rarely call. My silences spool out

like dropped thread. Of course, flight
occurs to me, but I live within walls.

I am the seat at the table borrowed
from another table. I was not invited.

Still, I know what etiquette calls for.
I can hear reason, dictating, in a nearby room.

I can hear the pencil scratching over paper,
taking every word of it down.

Ballroom, Lee Plaza Hotel

The grand is tipped on its side. Octaves old enough
to be ivory ascend into air that is empty of dancers.
The lid is missing, looted for some vagrant's fire:
African cherry or maybe East Indian rosewood, crackling
into ash to thaw fingers. Treble strings, then bass, then
soundboard, tilt toward the ballroom's carved dome.
All else is blue rubble, dulled gold, glass shards made
glitter by the streetlamp through arched windows.

How do I stop myself from imagining the couples clinging,
twirling beneath the chain that once held a chandelier?
How do I ignore the woman who surely leaned in sequins
here across the glossy wood to shape notes that rose
and broke against mirrored light? Even in the stilled
shambles, something beautiful remains. Of all the images
of this aching city, this is the one I keep coming back to,
the one that I send to you instead of words.

In Tongues

This is another tongue he doesn't speak, but then
he doesn't speak most tongues. She whispers it wet
and tremolo, and leans her head against his chest,
lets his baritone thrum a cadence through her hair.

I'm in here, he wants to say, pressing her cheek
hard to the white cotton of his shirt. The beat of her
reminds him of a stunned bird, and for a moment
he almost answers in bird, but refrains before

he can open his throat. When she pulls away
and lets her words dry in the air, he wants to water
them to save their shine, even though he still isn't certain
what they mean. Their shimmer helps him

glean something he thinks she wants him to learn.
He holds one to the sunlight, turning delicately
his fingers like a safecracker's, listening for a lock
to click or a catch to give way in his body. He dreams

of putting it in his own mouth, translating her into
a tongue they both might speak, but the pulse this
quickens in him is ragged and wild. Ashamed, he
drops the unbroken word back into the air,

presses her ear against the swirl of his own. *If
you listen hard,* he says, *you might hear an ocean.*
He imagines chart after chart he could yet unscroll;
she murmurs back in waves he longs to name.

Imperatives

Repot the plant on the kitchen sill. It has outgrown
the soil you gave it, and its roots hurt. Note how
the longer runners have forgotten which way to go
and strain now for the tap or the dishwater. Snap
them out of their misery. Save what you can.

Wipe the dust from surfaces. Unstack so you
can move without topple or dodge. Scour what's
stale with wind that smells of juniper and snow.
Open windows even to zero and claim its sting.
Hang words out to see if they freeze or thaw.

Don't wait for April, for it will have other plans—
pipers in uncurling leaves, lilacs to ache you, wet earth
to tease you from the house. Call a sweep to scrape
the creosote from your chimney bricks and send
the starlings in search of new nests. Light a fire.

Imagine the dream someone else is having. Wonder
why his lids barely flicker but his legs flail, and why
in the morning, the blankets are on your side. Stop
taking into your own lungs all of the moonlight that
splits the dark. Leave some. See what he does with it.

Without Snow

It is hard to wake to a world sharp with all of its old edges
after being promised that white muffler, that cold swath
of bandaging, that anodyne that would turn to blank

all that I am tired of feeling and, instead, scatter glitter.
But today looks exactly like yesterday. In this mottled landscape,
I know my place. All of the borders are clearly marked;

I will not transgress and do what cannot be
undone. What I crave in burial by snow are erasures—
miles of lines swallowed, navigation instinctive

and subject to error. Life is circumscribed, but not in
the old way. No one can be sensible when the earth
has disappeared. Even the honorable wear disguises.

If the world tilted crazily beneath a glut of white, no one
could blame me if I lost my footing, if I forgot myself
and became again that girl who'd topple backwards into

anything, who'd open her mouth to sky to give the icy
stars a place to fall and burn, who'd drive through a blizzard
with the top down just so you could see trouble coming.

Ghost Trees

The ghost trees bloom again.
At night they can no longer hide what
they truly are, bursting out of the blackness,
white and incongruous. Dirt is wet with
their secret, and the air tells it, retells it,
until I long for lull.

What I wouldn't give for the old stupor—
odorless null of ice-glaze, January's
mole-blind coma, stark and safe from sticky buds.
Instead, a heliotrope threading through my
bones, tipping me lightward, whether
to moon or meridian.

I stall at the car, unwilling to breathe
the house's slow anesthesia; I lean lung
and nerve into the air's conspiring. Each breath
sprouts a new thorn. The windows boil dull yellow
behind the motionless curtains. There is no one
anywhere to discover I'm still alive.

But wait—

All night the moon skulks the garden, illumines
answers you tell me mean nothing.

Look there, how fast the milkweed stabs
free of the dirt and prods the wet air;

how already, on the leaves' secret undersides,
monarchs have left beads of themselves.

Beneath the root-tipped flagstone, hundreds
of pill bugs wobble like tiny armadillos,

and over it, a slug scrawls flawless directions
of how to get from here to there.

Under the tool shed a possum, whose ancestors
walked with dinosaurs, licks the little beans

of her babies pouchward with a novice
instinct and waddles lawns lit by old light.

The lilac planted under the eaves, blossomless
for years, has grown sideways, and at the tip

of one straining branch, a pale bloom bobbles
like the sole survivor on a black sea.

A spider spins a penthouse that will lodge
bound wings by morning, and the stolons

of the honeysuckle have fastened on the earth
in kisses shuddering with new vines.

Stay with me here at the window. Look *harder*.
I'm telling you, nobody could make this up.

II.

Going Home

At twilight, I tug you down my childhood streets.
This is how it would feel if I could take you
inside of my dreams.

Here are the old houses, but moons
with different faces rise from the windows;
the long lawns are dappled with ghosts.

The saplings now sprawl, their limbs
scraping through clouds. Old trees
are not here at all: the hickory

that made me tiny, buzzsawed down
to stump—uprooted for a mouth
of stones, yawning delicate geraniums.

I am an oaf in the suburb
of Lilliput. The lout's boot
across unbroken snow.

I see it before you do—impossible
silhouette perched on the roof peak
of a gabled Cape Cod.

A great blue heron eclipsing the chimney,
stretching its wings across an orange sky.
How could it be here, you wondered,

so far from water and rookery, from the splash
of fish that risk their lives by breaking
the surface, by daring air? Taller from where

we stand than the radio tower or phone lines,
ancient bill open to swallow the sun,
it seems for a moment more monster than bird:

an archaeopteryx that bumbled on
a cul-de-sac. On a fist plucked bare,
a feathered thumb.

The Woman in the Window of My Old House

She watches over the azalea buds as though
they belonged to her, as though from her tight
knuckles sprouted my mother's green thumbs.

I see clearly each bone and hollow of her face,
now that the hickory that shadowed our lawn
has been amputated to stump,

now that all that passes over the yard
are jets, power lines, and, occasionally, birds
on their way somewhere warmer.

Does she know that she is living
with ghosts? That each evening at six,
my father passes through her foyer and calls

my name? That the low murmur she takes
for neighbors is really David's Psalms or
the Book of John incanted in a Southern drawl?

This is not the first time she has spotted my car.
Does she take me for an earthly threat? The tilt
of my pale face above the steering wheel

holds her in a beam of uncertainty:
something in its shape reminds her of the child
that has watched her from the top of the stairs.

The Air Then

The air then was more amber and there was hickory in it.
Wild bees lived in the ground and swarmed, and our feet
were often in the branches, our faces in the green and yellow
dappling that flickered as the wind blew through.
We pushed baby buggies and bicycles over grass so long
it lay flat in the wet heat. We watched boys hop and fall
from a black train that came before we knew where it was going.
The air was full of mothers and charcoal burning and bells.

Pianos played from the open windows and insect wings beat
in our hair. Shade was a dream that smelled of moss and stones;
on asphalt crisscrossed with rolling balls, tar bubbles rose and fell.
Green apples dropped to the front lawn and tanged the afternoon.
At dusk the dark welled with lightning and roses. Voices moved
without bodies in the shadows; laughter warbled through the spinning
blades of fans. The air was too heavy to leave the night that held it;
our lungs filled again and again, and each time we let it go.

How It Began

We didn't need to steal apples.

My mother kept the plaid bowl full
of Empires, Jonathans, Granny Smiths
and Galas, and had we come inside
for a break from kissing in the green cave
below the azaleas and rhododendrons,
we could have had as many as we desired.
It was instead because of the tree set back
from the road, the padlocked gate, the prickly
old man who wasn't that day rocking on
the squeaking porch swing, the story we were
already learning about who were the doers
of bold deeds and who were the watchers.

The boy scaled the chain link, dropped
into high grass and dandelions, fell to
his belly and wriggled down the deep lawn
while I peeked from behind a hedge of thorns.
He was in the crook of the crabapple, reaching
for a second time when the shot cracked the air,
scattering crows, setting blocks of penned dogs
to barking. Another shot, another, and the boy
was halfway down the yard, the one thieved
prize clutched in his fist, the croak of
the watchman at his back—*Stay the hell away
from my apples*—and as he cleared the fence

and fell against me, his sweaty body beating
and gulping air, a final cry—*I see you,
missy. You're as guilty as he is.* We ran
until we reached the alley, sliding down into
gravel below a tool shed's low overhang.
Swirled dust fell and stuck to our damp skin.

He handed me the apple, small and hard,
punctured already by some intruder, and I took
a tiny bite because I had no other choice.
We were through with kissing. The late gold
of the afternoon filled with supper bells and we
went back to our lives. This was the first

of my thefts—and the only one with gunfire.

She Fled

She fled, on foot,

            her baby in one arm, a brown grocery bag spilling
clothes in the other. The screen door banged behind her and made
all of us look up from kickball, through the gnats and wet August air,
to where she turned our street into a movie, the kind we'd never
been allowed to see.

            Before we could pivot, glance
at each other, we heard the second slam, saw her husband standing
on the stoop, hair frantic, a rifle with a telescopic sight clenched
in one fist. She saw him, too, and made a sound that seemed
less sob than moan,

            tried to run faster, spilling colors from
the bag she carried, leaving behind her a trail of tiny shirts, a flowered
skirt, a pink brassiere. I want to say that he shot the gun—peered
down that scope and fired—because in my memory, this is a story
of a man who used all

            the weaponry he had, but truth be told,
he never had to pull that trigger. He covered the ground
she'd gained in seconds, shook her hard by the arm that held
the bag, which tore and spilled more colors, as well as the folded
squares of cotton diapers,

            and then yanked her back down
the street, she and the baby, both crying, her face gray,
her son's purple. From start to finish, it took no more than
two minutes, and then their door was closed, so we could only
listen a long while to the hot

            voices, noises, that escaped their open
windows. The clothes stayed in the street until someone's
mother gathered them and laid them, folded, on their steps,
then turned and told all of us, firmly, *Go home,* and so
we went. I wondered, after,

                    where that woman thought
she had been going when she tore up the street to what seemed
like nowhere, her neat house and yard behind her—
if she thought then that she, too, was going home, instead
of fleeing it.

That Sanderson Show

There was nothing even remotely sexual in what we were doing,
so you couldn't call us voyeurs or Peeping Toms. It was closer

to eavesdropping, though we couldn't hear a word, could only
watch. It was reality TV with the sound turned down, long before

reality TV was invented. And so we called it "The Sanderson Show,"
sneaking up to my parents' bedroom after dinner to peer out

of the dark room at the house next door. Nothing about
the Sandersons was riveting, except what made them

watchable in the first place: not a single curtain or blind, at least on
the side that offered itself to us like the belly of a submissive animal.

Our perch gave us a split-screen view of the living room, the den,
the master bedroom and the son's room. If anything racy transpired

between Mr. and Mrs., it happened long after my sister and I had gone
to sleep, but in that season that ran one long and snowy winter,

we watched our fill of sibling spats, cocktail mixing, the boy's
struggling reps on a chin-up bar. To jazz things up, sometimes

we'd call their number to watch them listen to us breathe,
or if we were feeling bold, we'd play some prank to unnerve

Mrs. Sanderson, who favored an armchair by a window directly across
from our line of sight, and could be tormented with unexpected

thuds or splatters that we contrived with tennis balls or well-aimed
squirt guns. But mostly, we simply watched, followed their patterns

from room to room as they moved, unaware that what they took to be
the sanctity of their private lives was far from private. Or sanctified.

Perhaps it seems disturbing, even eerie, this fascination we had
with the Sandersons, but I saw myself not as perverse but, rather, a spy

or an anthropologist, noting for later reference that not all dull people
hid some sordid secret or covert wickedness. Sometimes they were just

dull. But I'll come clean. It was also a little like being God, a small taste
of something I imagined was power. It was being for a brief while the knower

of all things, the keeper of the dark side of a satellite, the seer of what happened
behind the walls that kept me out and behind those that still kept me in.

Missing the Train

Every Saturday at five
in my basement den,
I had a date with Don Cornelius
to ride the Soul Train
to funk.

Teetering in my platforms
and hip-hugging bells,
I was a shining star, the brick house
of a Commodore's
bass dream.

I shimmied, bumped and boogied
in flickering blue light,
practicing moves that would mesmerize
faceless men out there
waiting.

In the mirrorless gloom, my
groove thing was flawless.
I was diva of dazzle and dance,
goddess of sex and
simmer.

Night played a backbeat promise.
This dance or the next,
Mr. Big Stuff with his badass 'fro,
rubber band grace and
gold chain

would discover me at last.
We'd get down in swirls
of wet smoke and stuttering strobe lights.
Every Saturday:
same dream.

Alone, I was a stone gas,
strutting down the line—
fist raised as Don wished me peace, love, soul.
White girl brimming with
black pride.

By night I'd be me again.
Furtive toe-tapper.
Corner-hugger too timid to buy
her first real ride on
the train.

Basement

No matter how many vagrants gathered deep below
the road, huddled along the creek to watch
a girl ride her bike over the roots of
the ravine into their secret

colloquies, or how many tattooed and slick-haired
men parked their pickups on the overhang
and shimmied down to the red clay
recesses on either side

of the tracks to drink beers too close to the rush
and sparks of trains, or how many of the boys
from the rented bungalows crossed over
the rails to look for easy marks like me,

the house was a womb that could be returned to,
and the basement was its cool, unseen interior
without windows to let in August
or grownup eyes.

There were cellar spaces I would not enter,
because of the way they breathed,
the sounds they beat with,
the gazes they held

in their empty air, but I spent hours at the center
on too-hot days, both the damp and dress-up
clothes around me—my mother's barely
worn red satin slip, the bolero

jacket and costume pearls, my grandmother's
hats with netting to cover my eyes and hide
whatever I could imagine doing in
the world beyond my door.

The Boys of Woodlawn Park

Boys spun from the rope swing to the humid
tangle of the creek, skinning shins on roots that twined
the banks, slicing feet on rocks and green bottle glass.
They let me swing, too, though I never let go
of the knot, but kept fists clenched as I circled
the water, long hair trailing behind in lank streamers,
new breasts pressed hard against last year's shirt.

Boys sat on the sewer pipe, smoking Marlboros
and licked-tight joints, cutting with old pocket knives
into shoulders, then tracing the sudden red to make blue
ballpoint cannabis-leaf tattoos that I knew would surely
poison their blood. They let me smoke, too, and I took
shallow puffs, breathing scent, not smoke, letting bare
feet dangle over the murk that bred below.

Boys dragged a stolen sofa down rocks
to the sewer's mouth, shoved it through to where
the tunnel budded in a wider bloom they christened
theirs. Hidden within it, they drank their fathers' beers,
clutched centerfolds, took turns with girls like Trinket Doyle.
They beckoned me, too, but I hung back, leery of that
narrow gloom, the stories unfolding there, retold in school.

They were only mine in the afternoons, when late sun
slanted long shadows over the slide and the jungle gym,
when air was thick with called names, scents of dinners roasting.
Night penned me up behind safe doors, where only an open
window would sometimes snare the sound of them reckless in
an unlit world. From that breeze as it turned outside the screen,
I composed my dreams of unknown, unknowable boys.

Wednesday, Mt. Olivet

We were sixteen and stole
into the house of God—he, certain here
no eyes could see, and I, steeped in hymn
and litany, still imagined from call, a response.
I led him to the balcony and the cherry curve
of the pew, its smoothness against our hot legs—
his, I imagined, the legs of Gabriel, covered
in coiled blond and the dream I resurrected
every night of my cheek, my mouth, across
those humid curls. I ached to lay on hands.

He was godless, and so I gave him mine,
murmuring creed and psalm into the hushed cool,
the late afternoon sun staining our faces in deep
reds and blues, in bottle-glass green. The air
was full of tissue-thin pages turning motes
in circles, of chords held in the tall pipes,
of the scent of him rising as easy as sparrows.
He said my name, my whole name, and because
it echoed, he said it again. I offered his back
to him—a confession of longed-for sin.

I had gospel to share, but didn't. Instead, I heard
his tale of church. How, once, moved to drop
coins into a poor box, his mother had stayed his hand,
snapped, *the poor will never see your money.* I wanted
to refute this, to silence him with my tongue, to sift
through yellow hair and salt for what was buried there,
for which I would have sold all that I owned. But
a pastor appeared from a darkness we had forgotten,
shooed us to the street with what would become
a prophecy. *Move on,* he said. *You can't stay here.*

Writing Memoir

        I set out to rebuild you from old parts:
a flare of sunlight tangled and burning in your wind-
ruffled hair; a bicep flexed and hardened by fingers
pressed deep into six steel strings;
and somewhere still

        a mouth that never met
with mine. I would place it now where mouths go,
tip my own toward it to see if the past could be
undone—or if the knot had been left too long, too
tightly cinched in freeze and thaw,

        in orbit and neglect.
From broken pieces of a year, abandoned bric-a-brac
stacked and teetering in the junkyard where I searched,
came rustlings and cries. This was the soundscape
of earthquake rubble,

        that eerie song listened for by
rescuers and their dogs. Something was still
alive there, though it defied all reason. Someone tapped
a small stone against a decade, and I couldn't tell
if it was you or if

        it was me. I had thought to bring you up
in pieces, to tinker and hinge, to make you a new tongue
and put words on it. But instead you came up whole
and leaned across me to type at my keyboard, so close
I could trace the blue tease

        of your veins, could smell cigarette smoke
and the glisten of skin from a long-gone day in June.
I meant to invent what I thought was you, then
put you back again. But the story is told now
and here you are—as resurrected as

any god, and harder to disavow.

Heirloom

My father's 1939 Royal I have hauled from one
house to another, its black bulk squatting beneath
browning fissures of its original cover.

When lifted, that cover crackles with grime,
delicate sprinkle of old dust to reveal
his loved machine.

Its scents of bygone ink, dried ribbon tattooed
with rhymes, rise and swirl—ghostly perfumes
unfolded from the dark bureau of childhood.

He comes back to me in the click of keys:
a jazz I forgot I knew until its staccato riffs
rattle the desk. Here again is the lullaby

that played through the walls and in my dreams.
These keys, worn into shallow bowls, hold
stories he pressed into them.

In this séance to summon a man, a girl, I let
my fingertips rest in the smooth hollows.
The keys clack dry, invisible font,

but I type on in charades of words, writing
the message that only he can read.
Into the tapping, deathwatch hours,

with spirit hands and ancient Royal,
I bluff the silence to channel
a story still waiting to be told.

III.

Goings and Stayings

We could not pack the ghost and bring her with us;
the not-fully-departed attach to houses—not

to people. It was not to us that she returned, but
to her room, the air in it that she had not yet

finished breathing, the body she had left rocking
in the chair lit by a known moon. This is why,

when my grandmother lifted the quilt, slid
into the bed my mother had taken as her own,

she said not a word, did not even glance at
her daughter. This is why when my mother turned

on the lamp and called, *Mama,* no one was there
who could answer back. And so my mother rose

and sat all night in the bright and humming kitchen,
waiting for us to wake and make her feel real again,

to hear this story that made a lie of that heaven story
I'd taken as true. My mother lived beside her own

mother for another ten years before we boxed that
old life and drove away—the garden behind us heavy

with blue hydrangeas, one window gleaming with late
sun to mark a room that was not yet tenantless.

Ghosts

Ruby, the Ghanaian woman who takes cares of my mother, believes
in the spirits of the dead—in ancestors one pours a drink for

at the dinner table, in bad ghosts who return to terrorize
the living and must be appeased with some small sacrifice. And so

when my mother begins speaking to a man she says comes in and out
of her room, opening and closing the drawers, scattering her papers,

Ruby edges uneasily toward the door. *You're scaring me, ma'am,*
she says, but it doesn't stop my mother from testifying to what she sees—

not only the drawer-banger, but also my grandmother and Jesus,
who, if you ask her, is *a very nice man* and makes her feel much better.

I like the idea that when I visit her, we are not alone in that room, even
though I suspect it is just us and the dust motes, just us and the air

that we pass back and forth between us. Still, there are ghosts to spare
in other places: this legacy of paper faces bequeathed to me, glued

onto tattering black or left loose in the clasp of a breaking spine.
I scan them into a new century, resurrect edges from blur, shadow

and light from yellowing. Each of them offering themselves to
that lens, making that desperate lift of a chin to say, *Look,*

here I am. I was here. I am tender with all of them, but the ones
without names make me ache. Wouldn't they long to slam

a drawer or two, fling beads and envelopes to make me bring them
back again? This brittle year is almost at an end, and I long

to forget. But there are those who won't let it happen easily:
my mother's restless visitor; these ghosts trapped in sepia and ovals.

The California Years

Alabama she left behind her like a cracked shell, the meat
of the nut long gone. To split the seams of an old self
and not repair it is a kind of fortune-telling.

From the tiny bungalow on stilts, my mother drove west—
turned her back to Union Springs, to the Coosa River,
to magnolia and cyrilla, and travelled toward all that

remained of her husband. Both bride and widow, she went
to bury these identified parts, and stayed ten years.
Did the South evaporate from her skin then with

the Santa Ana winds—the muggy dew she wore like any
good belle of Dixie, parching, then twisting through a wildfire
in the San Gabriel Mountains? Did she sunbathe

on terra-cotta tiles, run her hands along stucco and drink
from trumpet blooms of fuchsia with the hummingbirds,
her heart quickening simply because it could, because

she was still alive? Now, at 90, she never talks about
that decade, the war, the streets petaled with jacaranda
blossoms, the nights brassy with Big Band and uniforms.

In a picture taken at the Hollywood Canteen a year after
her first husband's death, my mother looks up beneath
eyelids heavy with desire, and waits to be asked to dance.

Dreaming Alabama

I summon to my tongue Tuscaloosa. Opelika. Eufala.
Then Tuskegee. Wetumpka. Talladega. Swirl the muddy
tang of the swollen Coosa River. The double-named dead
of my childhood: Miss Jenny, Eva Catherine, Idonia Lee.
Hum of hymn, of the friend I have in Jesus. I roll a drawl
through bourbon and julep, drone the litany of all my blood.

I dream heavy voluptuous air, asphalt that steams
after downpour, dust swirls, dirt roads printed in toes
and hound paws. In a pick-up, I track pit stop barbeque,
ramshackle honky-tonk, river delta. To jukebox and twang,
a two-step insists, a fistfight always in the offing, sweating
bottle on a chipped bar, a man who will call me Darlin'.

I conjure wisteria. Magnolia. Spanish moss foreshadowing
sin and its jubilee. Hellfire. The Holy Ghost of Gulf
and shrimp gumbo. A Christ haunt from Dothan to
Birmingham. Through my mama's Montgomery, a march
of gospel and burning. Wings and the risen above Mobile:
Pelican. Cormorant. Impossible great blue heron.

The Naked Days

The house then was a clearing of white light,
bordered by a forest no one knew how
to move through but the three of us.

This was after and before there were men.
This was the lull we called alone. Now when I
want to conjure that time, I try *wind, wood smoke,*

wet earth, wolves. My daughters moved
on all fours, hair scented with fallen oak leaves
and torn branches. Nothing was quiet except

the world outside us. We opened our mouths
and could breathe the moon. This was after
and before. Now the older tells the younger,

Remember the naked days. Those days
when they wore their bodies unfathered,
unbrothered; when they lived in their skin

with their fast hearts, their lengthening bones.
Then I lived with no one in my bed, the wide
sheets as undisturbed as a sea I did not have

to cross. When I rose, I was their mother.
Their other. We were three and all. We named
ourselves with more than one name and balanced

each on our tongues, gave them as offerings
to the forgiving air. For a time that didn't
last, we let ourselves answer to all of them.

Mercies

My mother used to tell me, *it's a mercy we don't know
the future.*

Who could linger in a kiss, run the tongue along summer's
saltlick, the fingers over the cinching of two bodies, if we knew
how autumn would untie that knot, how the salt would lose its taste?

Who could toast to a new year if we knew all that it held? Hours
before an accident, a father wipes icy lace from the windshield
and presses it like a gift into his son's hand. A woman laughs

on a cell phone, buys a thick paperback before the boarding call
to a plane that will not take her home. But when the minister
dropped by the other day to sit with my mother, she knew enough

to ask us, *Am I dying?* And we knew enough to tell her, *no.*
Days now after the blizzard that took two samaritans, that left strands
of dark, cold houses closed fast around those who couldn't leave them,

that gouged a ragged, gravel-pocked gash into my new car, I look
out my bedroom window to find my house has become a weapon.
From the eaves hang uncanny, 12-foot fangs of ice, each dripping

into tips as whittle-deadly as stilettos, aimed at the unbroken snow
of the back lawn. They glitter, eerily lit by streetlamp, while
I lie, unsleeping, staring out at a new landscape through

my home's bared snarl. I could get up now, crank open the glass,
knock them, javelin-swift and spent, impotent, into tenantless
white, but I do not. I leave them to fall in their own time.

        It is also a mercy that we can know
the future and live on, matter-of-factly, as though we do not.

Those Mothers

You hear of them, the teller suddenly dismissive
or snide or welling in a venom that chokes the voice.
These are the mothers who botched the job so badly

that they are abandoned along the side of the trail,
too heavy to be carried out of the canyon.
Deadweights. Millstones. A leak

of muddy river bailed from a swamping boat.
A harpy set adrift on an ice floe.
I never planned on becoming one of them.

I used to pull a chair up to her crib to watch
her sleep, to wonder at the way the small lungs knew
what to do without my having to instruct them.

For years, I read to her in her twin bed, waiting
for questions that rose out of a place so old
that neither her father nor I had ever been to it.

And for years, our house tilted in its plot of earth—
groundwater swelled, breaking levels of concrete,
patterns of stones—but slowly, and so we tilted with it.

There was no one day when everything changed.
There were so many days that I couldn't count all
the steps she was taking backwards, away from me.

In These Woods

Pretty viper, once coiled
in my belly's fist, harmless
as a pinkie toe—now you lengthen
to dart, all lip-lined
fang and venom.

In these woods I step
blind over logs, unsettle
boulders, thrust a clumsy
stick into dark caves
to find you, to run my lonely
fingertips along the sequin-dazzle
of your low slither.

I would charm you if I could
with shiny baubles,
a shoebox of all the old gifts:
creeksplash over moss-slick
stones, a teacup of blue-black crickets.

But I am clatter and stomp
in this green quiet. Instinct
tightens you to tremble and strike.
In the bloodbeat before
each bite, I marvel
at your taut grace—swell
with pride at the honed arc
you master to carry
fang to heart.

Bound

Your first night in the world
I stayed awake to watch
the rise and fall of your
small ribs, the pink blanket
over you as it arced and hollowed.
I knew as certain as wave
to moon, your lungs
would not fill without my vigil—
that the frail stitch of your bones
was pulled only by the needle
of my gaze.

All these years later, you think
that thread has frayed
to the point where it can be
broken, that the splaying ends
unravel, that you can be
free—and do not see how
our helices twist like kudzu vines,
how they tangle and tie one
sorrow to the next—unmindful
whether they are yours or mine.

Advice to a Mother

Look away. Instead,
tip your face into the pardon of blue,
the twirl of wood smoke from a rooftop
behind you. Breathe air that has never
draped across her shoulders.
Pry loose the tight snails
of her earliest fists.

Look away and do not look back
until the blackened vine throbs green.
Until your ears do not
thrum with the wings of katydids
and over water you can skip
the flat stones of her eyes.
String the long days from a wind chime.

Wait until the weathervane
stops spinning;
look back when you can draw a circle.
Watch your rag doll
grow bones and wobble
out the door in her goodbye shoes.
Her fishhook pulled
from your tongue will jangle
on a bracelet of charms
only you would wear.

Your Oak

It sprouted your first spring with stubs of Kentucky Blue,
with breeze-blown seeds of zoysia, and grew faster
than milkweed, but only at night, so that every morning
we woke to a new-made thing, a creation that had never
been in our yard before. Without agreeing on it, I took
no loppers to its bark, your father mowed carefully around
its grey spear and sticky buds, until it overtook the rusting
wire fence, the roof of the car and then the telephone line.
It changed from oak into green shade flickering, and shadowed
you on your swing, in your furrows and mountains of sand.

Now, after nineteen years, I look up into its limbs that toss
and alter sky. The tip is a stone that parts a pond of blue;
the waver of wind through the leaves are ripples that widen
out from that stone. The first of the ripples is gone.
From a distance one sees how the tree grew at a tilt, not
heavenward, but leaning into the house, sidling up to
its windows and rubbing its shimmer of jade or brown
over the bricks, the panes, the way a cat butts it head
into a hand that will love it. At night the tree teases the glass;
it shivers and sighs on gusts of all that is left of a hurricane.

The Tree Leans In

In any downpour, and certainly in this slow-moving
hurricane, the tree leans in and harasses the house—
a green thug, long arms smacking at the porch roof,

the dripping panes. The air beyond the window
has been shifting for hours and the tree has been
swayed by it, bows to a new malevolence and bullies

the bricks I use to keep me sound and whole. The lull
of what I thought I knew gives way to a pitch and snap
of limbs that seems outside the laws of the physical world.

I see I cannot count on anything. The roots may even
now be loosening in the soaking ground, letting go
of their tenuous grasp of dirt gone mud, ready to give

the tree up to the tilt of this earth, to its final
embrace with the house. I am in it alone. So many
empty rooms, but I sleep, or try to sleep,

in the one beneath these flailing branches.
This is not the first time I have watched the tree change
or the first time I have felt it watching me back.

IV.

With a Twang—Not a Whimper

While I will own my blues, my rock, my Motown,
will let anyone eavesdrop on a bar of Billie or
Marvin through the open windows of my car,
I am furtive with my country, that twang and steel
a twinge of shame. A hot secret.
Still, there is a tawdry kind of sorrow only

honky-tonk will answer. So when you tell me
you will be boxed and gone by the time I return,
I wish I'd packed me some Patsy or Loretta
to tide me through the long drive home. No words
are apt in moments like these except those sung
beside a bar, a bottle sweating in my clenched hand.

I came here to write poems. Instead, I am doodling
only titles for songs I'd like to listen to in a dark-
paneled roadhouse, belted out loud and heartachey
by someone beehived, with a back-up of Dobros
and cowboys in fancy shirts done up with snaps.
There, boots would tap to "I'd Tell You I Still Love You,

But Then You Might Not Leave." Couples would
two-step to "You Can Take Your Money, Honey,
But I Want Back Those Years You Stole." God knows
I've been in this bar before. Watched the dancers
twirl in seamless twosomes, every move a perfect
dovetail born from habit, from the sheer pluck to not

let go. In the corners, there are plenty like me who
beat time, but only watch. Whatever gets scrawled
on napkins here has always been scrawled before.
Push any buttons on a jukebox and then order
another round. We didn't stick it out. I reckon
someone's already written a song or two about that.

What's Waiting

I know what I will come home to: a quiet unlike
the quiet we have lived in for so long on our separate floors,
a quiet as deep as a well no one would dream of throwing
a penny into, a silence that cannot be interrupted by
the clinking of dishes and silver, by water moving
through walls, by the footsteps and key turnings
that passed for a marriage.

The bedroom will be bigger, the rug bluer in new
rectangles revealed by what you are taking:
dresser, night stand, wicker chest. Your office, which
held nothing of mine, will be an emptiness waiting
to be remade or left to spiders. I have lost track of all
that you brought with you, things I have held
for so long as my own that I have forgotten

they are not, but you will take pains to remember.
I will come home to a house now wholly mine—
plaster and brick complicit in the deed of hiding me.
This is the way tissue is reabsorbed by a body. This is how
footprints are swallowed by new snow on old. I have been
true to this house. It is a comfort to know, at last, that I
have held on to something that does not want to let me go.

A Day in August

This is the first day of summer's dying—
the sky, blanched and low, the breeze
cool enough to raise goose bumps.
August sends a warning, scatters
pale yellow leaves like a trail to follow.

The last day of our life together
has already happened, but it is this day
I will use as a marker, chosen for
its anesthetic white, its bleakness without
even the promise of a storm.

Fitting that we should go out like this.
No tears or accusations, no questions
asked that might actually be answered.
Hours pass because the clocks say
they must. Birds seem bewildered

about where to go. Without a sun
to spill itself across the late afternoon
before twilight comes, this parting
is bloodless. Any ruckus I might
have made would be unseemly here.

Checking the Weather in Barrow, Alaska

There is somewhere drearier than where I am:

early fog blurs a circling sun that neither rises nor sets,
and wind quickens to a pummel over treeless, greenless Barrow,
over *Ukpeagvik,* place where the snowy owls are hunted.

August and barely above a freeze, the brown Chukchi Sea
surprises itself by moving. Tideless, it stirs its improbable
living in the shadow of a beached bowhead's arched bones.

Tonight the sun will hide in flurries; tomorrow, in a gray rain
that will hang, revolve, for days, unnoted. The coastline is gravel,
black and gray. The permafrost, unbroken, is black and gray.

I check each morning to be certain Barrow suffers. I wait for gray
to flick from pewter to steel on the webcam, for the spattered
houses on stilts to expel their owners. The dirty flatbed in the lens

is always turning. Satellite dishes listen from the tundra's edge.
Only Barrow is bleaker than my own bleak mind—but any sensible
Inupiaq would tell you if asked, he'd rather live there than here.

Settlement

She will never leave here. How could I coax her to go
with me, to abandon the front stoop, hot with white light, or
the myrtle, ready to honor its pink covenant?

This is where she waits for the baby to cry, where she dries
her long hair and listens as notes thread through the screens.
This is the place where the dark days could not follow.

When I move, I cannot take her with me. Here I can still
slip inside her bones, close my eyes within a minute
that ticked by decades ago. But where I am heading

will never contain her. I will have to live there only in
this changed body that knows no other time, that has never
yielded at night to honeysuckle tangling outside

the window. I must learn to live in a narrower house—
must leave the oak that leans in to hold me here,
the geometries of green and sun shaking against the glass.

Will they sense her as she divides their air, walking along
the ghost walls that marked this property before it was
doubled? Their dining room is where her child will wake

from napping, waiting to be gathered back into the heat
and currents of an old world. Their den is where she will go
when darkness takes the rooms and where she will rise

when morning gives them back again. What I sign to
surrender this house will not disclose her, and yet she will
convey—a name scratched in bark, a scent that never fades.

Valediction

House, my days in you are numbered. Though
I have changed you to suit me, have moved
your walls and raised your roof, though

we have watched one another grow old,
I do not think I can stay with you much longer.
You ask more than I can give.

You knew me new and lithe, unencumbered as
an April limb against the pane, long before my
daughters' heartbeats disrupted the air inside

each room. You knew me whole and sound as
sunlight through a picture window, unbroken by
mullion or dulled by scarred glass. Later,

you saw me invaded—leaned over me, a solicitous
and undemanding god. Together, we have been abandoned,
have watched while what we permitted inside

left us, and while what we tried to keep out
came in. When you flooded, I bailed you dry.
When I faltered, you hid me from all

eyes but your own. I want to do right by you,
but when you fade or crack, I have no means now
to save you. I do not want to stay to watch

both of us weather and fail. Our bond will be
always volatile. I will hate whomever you take in
after I am gone, will imagine the many ways

they are making you no longer mine. What choice
then but that I stalk you? You will feel me just
beyond the darkness. Your foundation will tremble

with what it knows. Do not close your curtains
to me. Leave lamps burning in every window to light
all the hours I will squander in the past.

The Mail

Every day, at least one letter arrives with your name
on it, but more often, two or three. The stack begins
to spill across the teak, and the cats take to napping on

this island of white. I should call to tell you not
everyone knows you are gone. If you have posted
word somewhere, it may have gone astray. People

are out there, awaiting your reply. I believe you may
have won something; your broker seems anxious
to share options you have somehow been living

without. A lucky thing that I am here to save you
from missing anything critical to your conduct
of business in this world. I should call to notify you.

I should call to say the cats are keeping warm
all that demands your attention. And perhaps
to tell you that soon this house

that has received and held so much of what you need
to know will no longer be mine. That strangers
will find these missives meant for you—

will bear the burden for you that I have been
carrying for so long. No matter what we do
or whom we tell, there will be days ahead when

someone sends us messages we will not be here
to open. Asks a question we will never have
the chance to answer. Who knows now who might,

in some distant year, return to love us, with no
better envoy than the postal service to say we are still
waiting, to let them know where we have gone?

In Boxes

I took pains to pack my life
in boxes, and was surprised
to find it could be done.
For a while, after the movers
drove off, I took no knife
to anything, nor did I peel
away the tape to bring
the old world into this one.

Everything was here, sealed
and labeled, so I knew
in which box I could find
which year, and where the proof
of who I was before I became
this other woman could still
be pulled out and placed on
a shelf, pointed to and claimed.

There was comfort in seeing
the past contained, the excavations
already made and named so I need
do no more than touch one to say,
This is mine. It is hard to begin
to open them, to look for places
here to hold what I still cannot
believe can be gathered and seen.

It is safer, maybe, to keep them
bound, to not let these new walls
surround what was and confuse it
with what is. This new house that now
seems so unknown already holds
a past that belongs to me—one that
someone who comes behind me
will find can be fit into boxes.

These Walls

These walls have never shared a mirror with me before.
They stand back politely from my nakedness, comparing

it to the nakedness of the last woman they enclosed and hid
from public scrutiny, finding me different but just as needful

of their discretion. I brought this mirror from the old house
to the new, because it knows me, because it remembers

my flesh and muscles when they were tauter, when I preened
and loved my readiness with an abandon that should have

embarrassed me—but didn't. I brought it, despite its cracked
and broken edges, its framelessness, because I know what it is

to be irreparable, to be no longer of use. When I hold it,
I am careful. When it holds me, it seems to return the favor.

The walls begin to discover what needs discovering: this woman
they contain and the jagged mirror that contains all of us.

I am learning to let them know me. Between last summer
and this one, nearly everything has changed.

I look to the glass for something familiar—
this body, this house I will move from only once.

Synchronous

My trees tremble and pitch
in the edges of a storm that is just
now shaking Florida, though here
the world is still pierce-blue,
still full of gleam.

A block away, a man, crazy
from theft of love or property,
has holed up inside his childhood
home with a gun, has doused
himself with gasoline. For 24 hours,

the cordoned road has turned
the cars away, and the hard breeze
has beat with a red pulse. This wind,
these sirens, are as close as I
come to calamity, and they

are all around me. Today I live
inside of them, though they are
not mine. I breathe the quaver
of unstruck phosphorous and sulfur,
lull my little terrors in the rising

wail that wills me to slow down,
to pull over, to permit passage
to trouble's answer as it hurtles
by me, just as though it might know
what to do when it finally arrives.

Creed

In my father's mansion are many rooms.

Physics has been a comfort since I strayed
from God. Think instead, I am told,
of my life as a series of rooms

in a house. The one I just walked out of
continues to exist, even though I can
no longer see it. And I trust

that the one I will enter next is already
waiting to hold me inside of it, though
it is not yet visible. This I know

even if I have never been inside
this house before, because this is
the nature of houses. And when I lie

at night in bed in my upper room,
I like to think how the basement goes on
without me, dust motes settling

on shelves and waiting to swirl
at the opening of the door at the top
of the stairs. This is as close as I care

to come to scientific thought; if I do not
push my inquiry too hard, it seems
to suffice, though I do not forget

that houses burn, that trees cleave
beneath an axe of lightning and fall
through roofs, or that sometimes

properties must be sold. I have lived now
in three houses. I believe I go on in each
of them. And this is what passes for faith.

When You Come Home Now, You Will Need Directions

Head south and away from the myrtle opening its pink
body without us, from the driveway, buckling and root-ruined.

Take the car one last time around the circle, then turn
left, out of the cul-de-sac. Those two small girls watching

from the front steps will be trapped no more than a moment
in your rear-view mirror. Drive away from the years

that are over. I am waiting here in the future
with the cat. I left in the backyard the gerbil bodies

beneath their mud-taken markers. I left, also,
the buried time-capsule for the startled digger of some

as-yet undreamed garden. It was always intended
for eyes that were not our own. Leave them

to their discoveries. If you count the distance in traffic lights,
I am only seven away from the life you remember.

I am waiting for you beneath a maple that is not long
from going gold. Already its leaves are turning a color

that didn't exist the day before. No, this is not yet home.
But I am here. Let's call it a beginning.

Acknowledgments

The author gratefully acknowledges the editors of the following publications where these poems first appeared.

Alaska Quarterly Review: "Without Snow"
Atlanta Review: "Ballroom, Lee Plaza Hotel," "With a Twang—Not a Whimper"
Barrow Street: "In These Woods"
Carolina Quarterly: "Imperatives"
The Cincinnati Review: "What's Waiting"
Harpur Palate: "She Fled"
Journal of the Mothering Initiative: "Those Mothers," "Your Oak"
Massachusetts Review: "Mercies," "The Naked Days"
Moon City Review: "The Mail"
New Ohio Review: "Writing Memoir"
Nimrod: "In a Handbasket," "What the Neighbors Know"
Southern Poetry Review: "Dreaming Alabama," "Foresight," "The Air Then"
WomenArts Quarterly Journal: "The Visitors"

Cover painting, "Suburban Glow" by Shannon Riley (on Facebook as shannonrileyart); author photo by Jennifer Davis; cover and interior book design by Diane Kistner (dkistner@futurecycle.org); Minion Pro text and titling

About FutureCycle Press

FutureCycle Press is dedicated to publishing lasting English-language poetry books, chapbooks, and anthologies in both print-on-demand and ebook formats. Founded in 2007 by long-time independent editor/publishers and partners Diane Kistner and Robert S. King, the press incorporated as a nonprofit in 2012. A number of our editors are distinguished poets and writers in their own right, and we have been actively involved in the small press movement going back to the early seventies.

The FutureCycle Poetry Book Prize and honorarium is awarded annually for the best full-length volume of poetry we publish in a calendar year. Introduced in 2013, our Good Works projects are anthologies devoted to issues of universal significance, with all proceeds donated to a related worthy cause. Our Selected Poems series highlights contemporary poets with a substantial body of work to their credit; with this series we strive to resurrect work that has had limited distribution and is now out of print.

We are dedicated to giving all of the authors we publish the care their work deserves, making our catalog of titles the most diverse and distinguished it can be, and paying forward any earnings to fund more great books.

We've learned a few things about independent publishing over the years. We've also evolved a unique, resilient publishing model that allows us to focus mainly on vetting and preserving for posterity the most books of exceptional quality without becoming overwhelmed with bookkeeping and mailing, fundraising activities, or taxing editorial and production "bubbles." To find out more about what we are doing, come see us at www.futurecycle.org.

The FutureCycle Poetry Book Prize

All full-length volumes of poetry published by FutureCycle Press in a given calendar year are considered for the annual FutureCycle Poetry Book Prize. This allows us to consider each submission on its own merits, outside of the context of a contest. Too, the judges see the finished book, which will have benefitted from the beautiful book design and strong editorial gloss we are famous for.

The book ranked the best in judging is announced as the prize-winner in the subsequent year. There is no fixed monetary award; instead, the winning poet receives an honorarium of 20% of the total net royalties from all poetry books and chapbooks the press sold online in the year the winning book was published. The winner is also accorded the honor of being on the panel of judges for the next year's competition; all judges receive copies of all contending books to keep for their personal library.

www.ingramcontent.com/pod-product-compliance
Lightning Source LLC
LaVergne TN
LVHW020938090426
835512LV00020B/3423